SandCastle 2

More Blends

ck

WITHDRAWN

Carey Molter

ABDO
Publishing Company

Published by SandCastle™, an imprint of ABDO Publishing Company, 4940 Viking Drive, Edina, Minnesota 55435.

Printed in the United States.

Cover and interior photo credits: Artville, Comstock, Eyewire Images, PhotoDisc.

Library of Congress Cataloging-in-Publication Data

Molter, Carey, 1973-
    Ck / Carey Molter.
       p. cm. -- (Blends)
    ISBN 1-57765-447-1
    1. Readers (Primary) [1. English language--Phonetics.] I. Title. II. Blends (Series)

PE1119 .M59 2001
428.1--dc21

00-056566

The SandCastle concept, content, and reading method have been reviewed and approved by a national advisory board including literacy specialists, librarians, elementary school teachers, early childhood education professionals, and parents.

Let Us Know

After reading the book, SandCastle would like you to tell us your stories about reading. What is your favorite page? Was there something hard that you needed help with? Share the ups and downs of learning to read. We want to hear from you! To get posted on the ABDO Publishing Company Web site, send us email at:

sandcastle@abdopub.com

Second printing 2002

About SandCastle™
Nonfiction books for the beginning reader

- Basic concepts of phonics are incorporated with integrated language methods of reading instruction. Most words are short, and phrases, letter sounds, and word sounds are repeated.

- Readability is determined by the number of words in each sentence, the number of characters in each word, and word lists based on curriculum frameworks.

- Full-color photography reinforces word meanings and concepts.

- "Words I Can Read" list at the end of each book teaches basic elements of grammar, helps the reader recognize the words in the text, and builds vocabulary.

- Reading levels are indicated by the number of flags on the castle.

Look for more SandCastle books in these three reading levels:

Level 1
(one flag)

Level 2
(two flags)

Level 3
(three flags)

Grades Pre-K to K
5 or fewer words per page

Grades K to 1
5 to 10 words per page

Grades 1 to 2
10 to 15 words per page

ck

Chuck likes picking fun things to do with his uncle.

ck

Becky likes wearing
her lucky shamrock
hat.

She has freckles.

ck

Brock wears a sack.

He has fun on the rock.

ck

My dog Bucko has a
black nose.

He licks the ice cream.

ck

Jack smiles as he blocks the slide.

His friends chuckle.

ck

Jackie kicks the ball
away from Mack.

ck

Micky fishes off the dock.

He brings a tackle box.

ck

These kids like to snack on chips and crackers.

ck

What does Vicki use to cook her marshmallow?

(stick)

Words I Can Read

Nouns

A noun is a person, place, or thing

ball (BAWL) p. 15
dock (DOK) p. 17
dog (DAWG) p. 11
fun (FUHN) p. 9
hat (HAT) p. 7
ice cream (EYESS KREEM) p. 11
marshmallow (MARSH-mal-loh) p. 21

nose (NOHZ) p. 11
rock (ROK) p. 9
sack (SAK) p. 9
slide (SLIDE) p. 13
stick (STIK) p. 21
tackle box (TAK-uhl BOX) p. 17
uncle (UHNG-kul) p. 5

Plural Nouns

A plural noun is more than one person, place, or thing

chips (CHIPSS) p. 19
crackers (CRAK-urz) p. 19
freckles (FREK-uhlz) p. 7

friends (FRENDZ) p. 13
kids (KIDZ) p. 19
things (THINGZ) p. 5

Proper Nouns

A proper noun is the name of a person, place, or thing

Becky (BEK) p. 7
Brock (BROK) p. 9

Bucko (BUK-oh) p. 11
Chuck (CHUK) p. 5

Jack (JAK) p. 13
Jackie (JAK-ee) p. 15
Mack (MAK) p. 15

Micky (MIK-ee) p. 17
Vicki (VIK-ee) p. 21

Verbs

A verb is an action or being word

blocks (BLOKSS) p. 13
brings (BRINGZ) p. 17
chuckle (CHUH-kuhl)
   p. 13
cooks (KUKSS) p. 21
do (DOO) p. 5
fishes (FISH-ez) p. 17
has (HAZ) pp. 7, 9, 11
kicks (KIKSS) p. 15

licks (LIKSS) p. 11
like (LIKE) p. 19
likes (LIKESS) pp. 5, 7
picking (PIK-ing) p. 5
smiles (SMILZ) p. 13
snack (SNAK) p. 19
wearing (WAIR-ing) p. 7
wears (WAIRZ) p. 9

Adjectives

An adjective describes something

black (BLAK) p. 11
fun (FUHN) pp. 5, 9
her (HUR) p. 7
his (HIZ) pp. 5, 13
lucky (LUHK-ee) p. 7

my (MYE) p. 11
shamrock (SHAM-rok)
   p. 7
these (THEEZ) p. 19

Match these ck Words to the Pictures

clock

socks

brick

pickle

24